Don't Quit Smoking, Drop One Cigarette

Unravelling My Tobacco Tale

JourneyTalesLK

JourneyTalesLK is the pen name chosen by the author for his debut book. His choice to withhold his real name while using a pen name is a unique approach rarely seen among authors.

However, He has interesting rational behind it ,Coming from a technical background with little exposure to literature, he never imagined he could write a complete book. His reading habits primarily focused on technical materials, driven by the belief that reading was solely for academic success and professional growth.

However, during his journey to quit smoking, he encountered transformative books that changed his perception of reading. He now embraces reading to personal growth and happiness, independent of others' expectations.

Undergoing significant personal development, he has evolved beyond his previous self. Now, he wants people to meet the new and improved version of himself as JourneyTalesLK. There may have been instances in the past where his nature might have caused misunderstandings, leading people to distance themselves from him.

He now desires to reestablish connections with everyone in his new persona, regardless of their previous opinions of him, confident that his fresh perspective can positively alter perceptions.

From the pen of the Author

As I embark on this journey, collaborating with Notion Press to bring my book to life fills me with pleasant surprise. Navigating this new realm of writing prompts reflection on my earlier days when I prepared for interviews to kickstart my professional career after completing my engineering degree. Just as I once crafted cover letters and resumes as a fresher, I now find myself doing the same, albeit in a different form — **crafting my Blurb and Author Bio.**

Back then, lacking experience to showcase on my resume, I hoped to attract potential employers. Now, as a debut writer, I find myself in a similar position, lacking experience in writing but aiming to captivate and engage readers, hoping they'll embrace me as an author. However, there's a subtle shift in perspective. In the past, success meant financial stability and a settled life. Now, it's about finding internal peace and genuine happiness.

I wish to dedicate this book to my beloved wife, who remains unaware of my decision to quit smoking and embark on this writing journey. I'm certain she will be pleasantly surprised when I reveal this secret to her as a special birthday gift.

Furthermore, I wish to express heartfelt gratitude to my close friends, who have served as unwavering pillars of support throughout these endeavours, particularly @shish & Praful. Former smokers turned successful professionals, they have not only provided encouragement but also offered valuable feedback on my early writings, spurring me to continue. They have remained steadfast by my side until the completion of this book.

I've come to understand that while many relationships are inherited, true friendships are earned by choice. To all those who have stood by me, offering unwavering support, I am deeply grateful.

To my readers, I extend an invitation to join me on this journey of self-discovery and transformation. May the pages ahead inspire, enlighten, and bring joy.

Contents

Contents

Introduction

About the author and the motivation behind writing this book.

Introduction

It is very difficult to start writing a book, especially when it's your first one, and crafting an introduction can feel daunting. However, this process is part of the learning journey, and like many others, I am also learning as I go along. I'm doing my best to articulate my thoughts within the pages of this book.

My motivation for writing this book is not to showcase myself as a skilled writer or to impart knowledge that you may not already possess. Instead, my primary aim is simply to share my own learnings and experiences with you. I hope that by doing so, you may find value in them, especially if they resonate with your own thoughts and experiences during your time as a smoker.

Allow me to introduce myself. I am an IT professional and Engineering graduate with close to two decades of industry experience. Presently, I hold a senior position at a well-regarded IT company. Despite my extensive experience, I do not occupy a top leadership role, as one might assume. Instead, I work in middle management.

You **may wonder why I mention this distinction.** The reason will become clear as you progress through this book.

In this book, **my goal is not only** to narrate my journey of quitting smoking but also to shed light on other crucial aspects of life vital for achieving happiness and reducing stress. Additionally, I'll share practical strategies I employ daily to manage stress effectively.

One piece of wisdom I want to convey is: '**Do not Compare**.' If you are happy and satisfied with who you are and able to sustain your position with your abilities and competence, do not compare yourself with others.

I am not suggesting that growth isn't important, but rather that it's important to grow at your **own pace** and according to your abilities. This approach will lead to happiness and reduce unnecessary tension, allowing you to focus on more productive things apart from your professional life.

I believe there's a strong relationship between smoking and work-life balance. When we experience fewer tensions and effectively manage the balance between our professional and personal lives, we tend to smoke less. Comparing ourselves to others or feeling pressured to be like someone, whether by our own standards or influenced by others, **can increase stress levels and lead to smoking more.**

I understand that individual experiences may vary, but upon careful observation, the root causes are often similar. **When you are satisfied and happy with who you are, you are likely to smoke less**. Therefore, all these aspects are interconnected. I will share more insights as we progress through the next chapters.

Why You Want to Quit?

Exploring the internal factors of individuals of quit smoking.

Why You Want to Quit?

If you're reading this book, it means that the thought of quitting smoking has crossed your mind. Perhaps it's your first time considering it, or maybe it's been on your mind multiple times before.

Like many, you've likely attempted to quit before. You've watched motivational videos, read articles and books, and sought advice from those who have successfully quit. You've given it your all, and you may have even gone without smoking for a day, a week, a month, or even a year. But somehow, you found yourself **lighting up again**.

Don't worry, you're not alone. Many of us have had similar experiences. Despite our efforts, we find ourselves back in the grip of the habit or you can say an addiction.

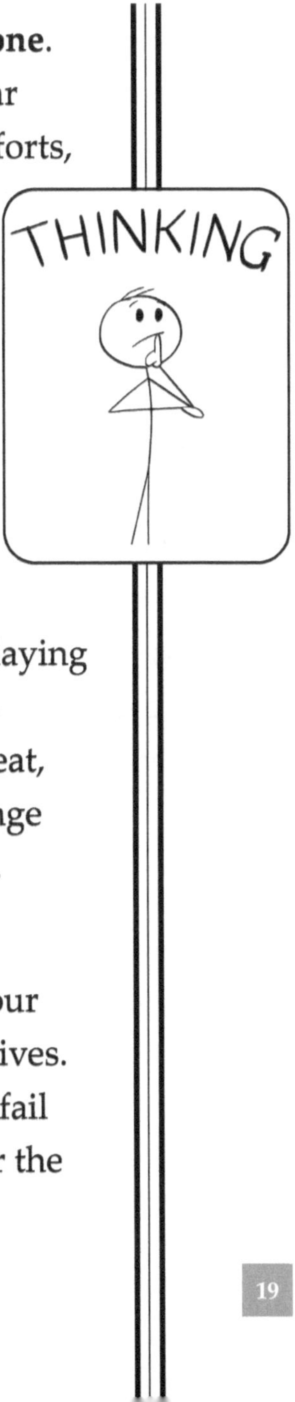

Yet, here you are, turning the pages of this book once more. It speaks volumes about your resilience and determination. You're displaying the true spirit of a fighter— refusing to succumb to defeat, ready to take on the challenge once more to quit smoking.

As humans, we encounter similar challenges in both our professional and personal lives. We attempt, fail, try again, fail once more, but then muster the courage to give it another shot—and sometimes, that's when we emerge victorious.

Consider the many tasks in life that initially seem impossible. Think back to learning to ride a bicycle as a child, mastering the art of driving a car, or **summoning the courage to approach someone you admire**. These endeavours often require multiple attempts before we achieve success.

Additionally, there are countless other endeavours we pursue repeatedly, yet still struggle to conquer. Whether it's strumming chords on a guitar, organizing documents meticulously by date, or perfecting a dance move, failure is a common companion on the path to mastery.

But at the end of the day, there's satisfaction in knowing that we've given it our all. **Failure is not a mark of shame; it's a testament to our courage and resilience.** If, despite setbacks, we continue to persevere, then there's always the possibility of triumph in the next attempt.

Now, let's focus on the main topic of this chapter. First, it's important to figure out why you want to quit. Don't quit smoking just because someone else wants you to, like your girlfriend, wife, parents, or someone you admire or care about, or because you've seen someone else quit.

Through my own experiences, I've realized that while loved ones can influence us to some extent to change habits, whether good or bad, as we mature, most decisions about our lives become our own. We face the consequences of these decisions and develop the internal resilience to resist changes that are forced upon us from outside.

It's possible that you may attempt to quit smoking due to external pressure, but I assure you, the journey will be more stressful and potentially more dangerous than simply having a cigarette. Therefore, I urge you all to consider that if you truly want to quit, **it must come from within, not from external sources.**

Advantages & Disadvantages of Smoking: Conduct Your Personal SWOT Analysis

Explaining how individuals can do their own SWOT Analysis.

Advantages & Disadvantages of Smoking: Conduct Your Personal SWOT Analysis

You've likely read extensively about the **disadvantages** of smoking, such as its link to cancer, breathing issues and problems in sexual health. However, I want to discuss the **advantages of smoking**, which I believe are crucial to consider when contemplating quitting.

As an IT professional, I'm familiar with the SWOT analysis method. Those who are not familiar it is self-analysis in which you can gain insights into your current situation, identify areas for improvement, and develop strategies to maximize your strengths and opportunities while minimizing your weaknesses and threats. It's a valuable tool for making informed decisions and planning.

Before deciding to quit, I believe it's essential to conduct a thorough analysis of the pros and cons of smoking.

Don't you think this is the right approach? If, after this self-analysis, I determine that quitting smoking would be beneficial for me, then I'll proceed. Otherwise, I may postpone the decision for now and revisit it in the future. Who knows, my perspective may change over time. The important thing is that this decision is driven by my own convictions, not by external pressure or influence.

Before starting the advantages of smoking, let me share an interesting discussion that I had with my wife. She always insists that I quit smoking, and I know she is worried about my health. I respect her concern, and I believe that those who love and care for us always advise and help us to stop smoking and other bed habit which is not good for our health.

One day, as usual, she started discussing with me what I really enjoy about smoking. This time, she was in a good mood and genuinely wanted to understand the pleasure and satisfaction I get from smoking. I was also in the mood (because I had a couple of beers) and was looking for someone to whom I could discuss such topics. This was a golden opportunity for me, as my wife wanted to listen to my thoughts (a rare occasion in a husband's life).

Then I started explaining the joy of smoking and the benefits I experienced as a smoker for the last twenty four years. I explained to her that when it comes to taste and smell, it's the worst, and you always want to avoid such things. Sometimes, I even feel bad or avoid places that are filled with cigarette smoke, like small smoking areas in airports or bars/clubs, where many people are smoking in a very confined space. In those moments, while smoking, you think, **"Is this really so important to me that I'm having this in such a situation?"** However, this good thought disappears from my mind with lightning speed, the way it came to my mind. After finishing my cigarette, I just move away from that place and only think that there could be better places for smokers, not like this dingy one.

Have you noticed how rapidly the urge to quit smoking diminishes, shifting our attention towards finding more suitable spots for smoking once we've finished our cigarette?

Returning to the discussion with my wife, I once again began to explain my perspective. "**You see,**" **I started, "the taste and smell are undoubtedly unpleasant**. However, as humans, we always seek to improve our current situation and move towards something better.

I believe that smoking, or even just the thought of it, provides me with that temporary satisfaction, tricking my mind into believing that I'm in a better situation than I actually am.

The temporary relief I experience from smoking is perceived

by my body and mind as a 'reward,' leading to cravings for that feeling, even if it's only temporary. I'm not suggesting that this feeling can't be achieved through other means—indeed, you'll find that every human has this reward system, whether they smoke or not, or even in the form of other unhealthy habits. It's a tendency that develops over time.

You may wonder why smoking is often considered a preferred option. It's partly because it's somewhat socially acceptable, especially in workplaces, and it's readily available almost everywhere, providing quick relief or reward.

So, I'm not dismissing the role of nicotine addiction in this process, but rather emphasizing the significant role of the reward system ingrained in our minds. We seek to escape our current situation and feel different, seeking that sense of reward."

I continued, drawing parallels with other bad habits. "Think about any unhealthy habit,".

I added one item intentionally to this list as I know my wife has the habit of eating white chalk when see is tensed, "like chewing tobacco, nail-biting, eating white chalk, or excessive tea or coffee consumption. We gradually develop these habits, establishing a reward system in our minds. Whenever we're tense and seek relief, even if only momentarily, we reach for a cigarette or any other bed habit we have.

I paused, observing her reaction, knowing she would have a response.

Sure enough, she began to argue, "Don't compare apples with oranges."

She then explained, "I consume very little white chalk when I'm tense. It's a different kind of addiction, less harmful, and I can quit anytime."

I smiled slightly and nodded, deciding to end the discussion there with my wife. Her statement reminded me of my own initial thoughts when I started smoking twenty four years ago. I used to justify my occasional cigarette by claiming there was nothing to it, and that I could quit anytime. However, I'm still smoking, so it seems the reward system is firmly set in my mind and only grows stronger with time Unlike my wife, who still believes she can quit eating chalk anytime as it's not a habit, she doesn't realize that her body and mind have already perceived it as a 'reward.' She will crave for it when she's tensed and seeking temporary relief from the current state.

Let's delve deeper into the advantages of smoking. While they may differ from person to person, certain benefits are universally recognized. As discussed earlier, one advantage is the 'reward system' that our minds have developed over time. This system primarily offers internal satisfaction, or, in other words, a benefit experienced by smokers. What other **external factors or advantages** do we experience?

FOMO, or the Fear of Missing Out, represents our unease regarding not participating in exciting or enjoyable activities that others are enjoying. This fear often motivates individuals to start smoking, as they seek to join and connect with a particular group. This tendency frequently emerges during college or the initial phases of one's professional journey.

Another fascinating aspect of smoking is that individuals who engage in it **often perceive it as a conscious choice.** Despite being aware of its negative effects, they view smoking to assert control over their lives, a sense of ownership that may have been lacking in decisions influenced by parents, teachers, or loved ones. Additionally, it provides a form of social connection within the smokers' community.

In my experience, I've found that smoking has led me to form meaningful friendships, some of which endure to this day. So, if we consider meeting new people and enhancing social connections, smoking undeniably plays a significant role. **This, in my view, is a crucial advantage of smoking.** I've built strong relationships not only with my college peers but also with my seniors and colleagues in my professional life.

I want to **emphasize** that while it's entirely possible to foster strong connections with college mates and colleagues regardless of smoking, cigarettes often serve as effective **conversation starters.** They create common ground, particularly among smokers, and can facilitate interactions in various social settings. Moreover, there are specific places where smokers tend to gather during the day, providing additional opportunities for camaraderie and socializing.

One significant advantage that I believe smoking provides is companionship. When I'm alone and have nothing to do, a cigarette is my best companion. I never feel lonely when I have cigarettes in my pocket. Whether I'm happy or sad and want to spend time with someone without being judged, I think cigarettes do that job very well. So, whenever I consider quitting and have tried in the past, I always find loneliness or emptiness within me, which I really don't like.

Based on my understanding, here are the three main advantages that I believe cigarettes provide, which I have previously discussed:

- The monetary reward system and the perceived improvement of our current state when we smoke.

- Social security, or the fear of missing out on the camaraderie within the smokers' group.

- Companionship provided by smoking when idle or desiring solitary time.

So before starting the disadvantages of smoking that we all know, I want to share one more interesting discussion with my beloved wife, who always tries to convince me to quit smoking whenever she takes some wisdom from the **social media university**.

She explains to me that if I keep smoking, my lifespan will be 5 years shorter. I agreed and retorted, "So you're saying that if I die at 80 and don't quit smoking, I will die at 75?" **Correct,**

She agreed. Then I explained another illogical point to her: that these 5 years will be added to my life when I am old (75->80). By that time, most of my responsibilities and desires will either be fulfilled, or I won't have the energy to accomplish them.

So, the use of these remaining 5 years, which I saved from quitting smoking, would either be used to regret what could have been done better in my previous days or to be satisfied with whatever I achieved in my life.

Then I posed the question, "How do you feel about it? Are you inclined to seize the joys of life at this moment, or would you rather temper your desires now in exchange for the possibility of adding five more years to your life when you're older?

She became irritated with the question and abruptly ended the discussion, leaving me with a perplexing expression that suggested she deemed me **hopeless**.

I will leave this thought for you to ponder and determine whether my point is logical or nonsensical. My philosophy is to live in the present because dwelling on the past brings pain and worrying about the future creates tension; we can only truly experience and control the present moment.

Let's now discuss the disadvantages of smoking. I'm sure you're aware, and you can easily find resources with just a click on the internet. People around us often readily offer lectures to those who smoke, overlooking the multitude of other bad habits they may have.

We all know that smoking is injurious to our health and can cause cancer. However, smoking is not the sole cause of lung cancer; there are studies and cases where people develop cancer despite never smoking. Therefore, there are numerous other factors that can contribute to lung cancer.

In my opinion, it's a matter of luck whether you smoke and develop cancer. At that point, people around you may criticize you for not heeding their advice to quit smoking, and you may also feel regretful.

While smoking is a significant cause of lung cancer, there is also evidence linking previous lung disease, occupational exposure, drinking water containing arsenic, and indoor/outdoor air pollution to an increased risk of lung cancer.

Let's assume that smokers are fortunate and lung cancer is not the cause of our demise.

If you were blessed with assurance from **God** that you will not die from lung cancer, **would you still want to continue smoking?**

Would the thought of quitting smoking be permanently erased from your mind?

Just give a thought to the above scenario while reading this engaging conversation with my father, a qualified doctor who has never smoked. I've done my best, or you could say I've pretended in front of him that I never smoke, or I'm just a very occasional smoker who tried it only in college but isn't habitually hooked on this bad habit.

I must say, it's incredibly difficult to hide smoking from someone who has never smoked, and it's nearly impossible if that person is your father and an experienced doctor.

It's quite easy for them to guess that you've just had a cigarette from the smell, which is very unpleasant for a non-smoker. Even if you take all precautions like using mouth freshener, washing your hands, and applying perfume, sometimes saying you were just standing with a friend who smokes, and the smell is because of my friend and not from you.

As always, during my vacation back hometown, I make sure to go far from my house to smoke, ensuring that nobody sees me and reports to my father that his son smokes. It's quite a challenge for a me to find a safe spot in my hometown where I can smoke without the risk of being recognized and questioned, especially with remarks like, **"Aren't you Doctor Sahab's son?"**

However, where **there's a will, there's a way**. I managed to find a very secluded spot—a small shop where I observed that most people there were of similar age. It seemed they were there for the same reason I was, which is why I felt comfortable smoking there.

So, as usual, I returned home after having cigarette, and it was a coincidence that my father was sitting alone at that time, lost in thought. Feeling confident that I had taken all the necessary precautions after smoking, I joined him and began chatting to convey that everything was under control, mentioning casually that I had just come back from meeting an old school friend.

Upon hearing this, he smiled and continued our conversation, discussing other aspects of my life and sharing insights from the spiritual books he was currently reading. I felt reassured that I hadn't been caught, believing I had managed things cleverly and that he remained unaware of my recent activity.

Suddenly, my father began discussing the prevalent bad

habits of today's society, such as chewing tobacco (which is very common in my hometown), smoking, and drinking. He referenced some of his patients who suffer from diseases related to these habits. It became evident to me that he was aware of my smoking, although he chose not to confront me directly about it. He continued by reminiscing about his own medical college days, mentioning that some of his close friends used to smoke, with some having quit the habit while others still smoked.

He then shared an intriguing insight: while smoking doesn't necessarily guarantee an early death from a fatal disease, it can lead to various health issues after the age of 40 or earlier that gradually diminish one's quality of life. These issues include breathing difficulties, decreased energy, chronic coughing, throat problems, and manageable heart conditions, all of which **slow down the pace of life.**

A slower pace often results in feelings of depression and anxiety, as one struggles to find enjoyment in life. Conversely, a faster pace leads to a sense of happiness and fulfilment, with time seeming to fly by. He concluded by emphasizing that the decision of how to live rests solely with everyone. We must decide whether to live our lives at a **good pace or struggle with a slower**

pace, and accordingly align our habits—whether good or bad. Ultimately, the decision is ours alone.

Now, returning to my earlier question, which I prompted you to ponder while reading the conversation with my father: If you were assured by God that you would not die from lung cancer, would you still choose to continue smoking? Would the idea of quitting smoking be permanently removed from your mind?

I'll conclude this discussion here, leaving you with the contemplation of your decision. Whether you pass away at the same age as a smoker or a non-smoker, **the pace of your life will undoubtedly be faster if you live as a non-smoker.** The choice is yours, and I encourage you to make it after conducting a thorough SWOT analysis, considering the three advantages and only disadvantages of smoking that **slow down the pace of your life.**

Understanding Your Smoking Journey

Reflecting on where you began this habit.

Understanding Your Smoking Journey

Understanding the journey of the smoking habit is crucial, as every habit follows its own path. Let's delve into the concept of habits and their development, whether beneficial or detrimental before I start explaining my own journey because I believe this is a crucial aspect in understanding how any habit forms throughout our lifespan. In our daily routines, we engage in various tasks that demand time, energy, and mental focus. Some tasks become ingrained and require minimal energy, driven by our subconscious rather than our conscious mind - these are what we refer to as habits.

What's interesting about habits is their ability to conserve time, energy, and conscious effort, enabling us to direct our attention

towards new challenges. Take, for example, the simple act of brushing your teeth in the morning and at night. Does it demand significant effort? Quite the opposite - it's largely guided by your subconscious mind, allowing you to effortlessly multitask while your conscious mind remains unoccupied.

As we **repeat activities over an extended period, they gradually transform into habits.**

Two factors are pivotal in this process: the frequency of repetition and the continuity without interruption.

Repetition holds more sway than time; for instance, repeating an activity twice a day might take three or four months to solidify as a habit, whereas performing it ten times daily could establish the habit within a month or so. Repetition ingrains the behaviour into our subconscious, aligning our body accordingly.

In my journey as a smoker, I've made an intriguing observation.

I've noticed certain individuals in smokers' groups who join for a smoke only occasionally. It surprises me to see some of them smoke just one or two cigarettes a month or indulge in a few puffs during special occasions like office parties.

I admire their ability to effortlessly switch between being a smoker and a non-smoker. Despite my curiosity, they never return for smoking breaks, even after I've directly asked them about their smoking habits.

I find it perplexing how these individuals seamlessly transition between being smokers and non-smokers. To delve deeper into this phenomenon, I invited a few of these occasional smokers for a cup of tea or coffee, knowing that cigarettes often accompany these beverages. While waiting for our drinks, I lit up a cigarette and offered one to the occasional smoker.

He politely declined, stating that he doesn't smoke. I reminded him of a previous occasion where he smoked like a regular smoker. He explained that it was a one-time occurrence after drinking beer, and he doesn't smoke regularly.

He emphasized that smoking isn't a habit for him, but rather a conscious decision. He views it as a bad habit and refrains from repeating it for weeks or even months.

Then I realized that these occasional smokers enjoyed that moment of smoking with a conscious mind

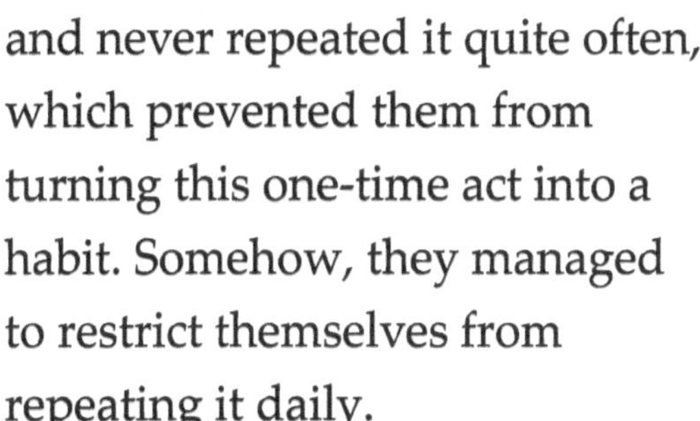

and never repeated it quite often, which prevented them from turning this one-time act into a habit. Somehow, they managed to restrict themselves from repeating it daily.

As I mentioned earlier, the repetition of the same act over time converts our activities into habits, whether good or bad. We often observe this when trying to develop a good habit; we may attempt it for a month or so but struggle to sustain or repeat it enough to solidify it as a habit. The same principle applies to bad habits. **Don't repeat them often, and they'll remain just a one-time occurrence on that day, eventually fading from memory.**

However, we must be cautious with bad habits, as they often involve chemicals with addictive qualities. It can be difficult to quit even if you repeat them only once a day for a week. Therefore, it's essential to refrain from highly addictive substances like drugs, as they directly impact your nervous system.

You might wonder why I'm sharing this without explaining why, how, and when my journey as a smoker began. The reason is that smoking, like

any habit, develops gradually through repetition over time. **Quitting follows a similar principle, requiring repetition and time to succeed.**

Let me tell you how, why, and when I started smoking. I joined engineering college in 1999-2000 at the age of 20. Before that, I had never smoked or even touched a cigarette. I came from a family where smoking and drinking were considered very bad habits, and I hadn't seen anyone in my family indulge in them openly. So, in short, I had no exposure to these habits and considered them very bad.

When I joined engineering college and stayed in the hostel, my room was shared with three people, one of whom had experience with smoking. He was familiar with this act of smoking and had been doing it since his school days. I'm not saying he smoked cigarettes in the room all the time, maybe just once or twice depending on the situation. Sometimes in our room, sometimes in other rooms with other first-year students who smoked.

Honestly, there were only a small number of individuals in my batch, encompassing all branches, with approximately

15% having some experience with smoking, and merely about 2% who were consistent smokers.

During the first six months of my first year, I never touched a cigarette and advised others not to smoke. However, during this time, I started to notice some of **its perceived benefits**. There was a special group in our batch who smoked, and they recognized each other easily, bonding effortlessly despite coming from different backgrounds, states, branches, or even other wings/ rooms in the hostel. I observed that this group also received attention from seniors who

approached them at night in search of cigarettes.

Externally, I pretended to not be inclined towards smoking, but internally, I was tempted to try it, not for the taste but for its **perceived benefits**.

Despite this temptation, I managed to resist smoking through my willpower. Then, one day, my roommate returned from abroad meeting his family as his father was posted outside country and brought back various interesting gadgets and items, including 3-4 packets of international cigarettes. All the smokers in the hostel were excited about this

and planned to enjoy smoking them at night since there were restrictions during the day and the risk of seniors confiscating them.

As my roommate, and with the new stash in our room, all the interested smokers from the hostel began to visit to check out the cigarettes packets, eagerly asking for one to enjoy later.

However, I observed all of this with a sense of detachment, unable to feel the enjoyment that the other smokers were experiencing upon seeing the packets of cigarettes.

During the whole day this was point discussion between in this group whenever they got a chance to discussion either in lectures, Labs, canteen and while coming back to Hostel from Collage.

That day was tough for me because I kept thinking that smoking must be very interesting, which fuelled the curiosity of others.

Eventually, at night, some selected smokers from that group, who were close to my roommate, came to our room to enjoy the puffs of those international cigarettes. While I was lying on my bed, listening to music with my Walkman, the moment everyone had been waiting for

arrived. My roommate opened the new pack of cigarettes and distributed them among the group. I watched as they eagerly lit up and took puffs, unable to resist the temptation any longer. **I jumped in with the group and asked my roommate to pass me a cigarette so I could try it too.**

My roommate and others were surprised and gave me strange

looks. Some warned me not to try it, but I was determined and ignored their advice. My roommate passed me an already lit cigarette, and I took my first puff. It was awful, and the taste was pathetic. After that puff, I was

genuinely surprised by what all the excitement was about. I expressed my disappointment with strong words, then asked for water and something sweet to change the taste of my mouth. I couldn't understand how they could enjoy it.

Some argued that it gets better with time, but I observed some experienced smokers who simply

smiled and enjoyed their puffs.
I believe they were reminiscing
about their first cigarette and the
similar reaction
they had, just like
me.

After trying
1-2 puffs of my
First cigarette,
I initially felt
confident that
I wouldn't smoke again due to
the unpleasant taste. Little did I
know, this marked the beginning
of my journey into smoking.

Despite disliking the taste, I
convinced myself that I could
simply pretend to be part of the
smoker group and enjoy the
**perceived benefits without fully
embracing the habit.**

As time went on, I found myself engaging in discussions with the **"smoking group"** and joining them at the canteen and other regular hangout spots. Initially, I limited myself to few puffs of the cigarette without fully engaging, believing I could quit at any time due to my aversion to the taste.

However, as I continued spending time with them, I began to experience the perceived benefits of smoking, which I secretly found myself enjoying. I started to view myself as clever for reaping these benefits without fully committing to becoming a smoker.

As previously discussed, repetition plays a pivotal role in gradually ingraining any act it habits over time. Unbeknownst to me, I had become a frequent participant in the smoker group, drawn primarily by the camaraderie it offered. Over time, **my subconscious mind began to assimilate these behaviours.**

Six months after my initial encounter with cigarettes, a noticeable shift occurred: I found myself unconsciously integrated into the smoking group, relishing their company. Throughout this period, I limited myself to sharing only 1-2 puffs or occasionally more, never committing to finishing an entire cigarette. By this point, my palate had acclimated to the taste of tobacco; while still not entirely enjoyable, it no longer repelled me as vehemently as it did initially.

I was completely unaware that I had fallen into the grasp of smoking. Up until that point, I had convinced myself that because I never smoked a full cigarette and simply enjoyed the company and perceived benefits, I wasn't really a smoker. It appeared simple at first glance. However, reality proved otherwise. Despite my conscious mind resisting acceptance, **I had undeniably adopted the habit of smoking through frequent repetition**. My subconscious had become attuned to the associated reactions.

This is how my journey of smoking started. Initially, for six months, I would take 3-4 puffs while sharing cigarettes with others. Over the next six months, I began buying 1-2 cigarettes daily with my pocket take few puffs on sharing basis with other smokers.

Despite my growing consumption, I remained convinced of my ability to quit at any moment of this habit.

By the time I completed my engineering in 2003-2004, my daily cigarette count had increased to four, which I bought from my pocket and rest taking few puffs with other smokers .In collage time most of the people are dependent on the money which they received from their parents so Due to financial limitation , we couldn't afford to spend much on cigarettes, which also contributed to buying fewer cigarettes.

I wasn't aware that smoking and drinking often go hand in hand, as I wasn't very engaged in drinking alcohol during my college days. Later in my journey, I realized that smoking and drinking alcohol make a **deadly combination**, and it's hard to quit smoking when you combine both.

After completing my engineering degree, I encountered the challenge of securing employment off-campus, as my college lacked robust placement assistance. I relocated to Delhi NCR and resided with a long-time friend who had recently begun working. He shared an apartment with a fellow MBA graduate who held a respectable position as an **Assistant Marketing Manager at a renowned cigarette brand.**

Having one of our flatmates employed at a cigarette company ensured **constant access to cigarettes**, despite my financial constraints. He frequently brought cigarette packs from his workplace to promote new products.

This accessibility deepened my involvement in the habit, particularly as my smoking frequency increased due to the stress of not finding stable employment.

After 6 months, I landed a job in a good company, but my salary package wasn't that great. However, I was relieved that I could survive on my own in

Delhi with that salary. Since my office was farther away from my previous place, I moved to a different flat with another good friend, who was a non-smoker.

I noticed a change in myself: my daily cigarette consumption decreased when I moved to my new flat because my roommate didn't smoke. Additionally, the free cigarette supply I was getting from my friend working in the cigarette company stopped. Until that time, I mostly bought cigarettes with my own money, considering my limited salary.

Almost 3 years have passed since I took my first puff of a cigarette. I found myself completely addicted to this habit, and now things have changed. I've started enjoying the taste of cigarettes, along with the perceived advantages I receive from smoking. While these advantages may differ slightly from those I experienced in college, they still hold some similarity, albeit in a different form.

Now, let's fast forward a bit in my professional journey. Over the course of twenty-four years, I changed companies and achieved a good salary while holding a respectable position.

After two to three years of starting my job, money wasn't an issue for me to buy cigarettes, and by then, **a "reward system" had developed in my mind along with the "perceived advantages"** I gained from smoking.

So, let me summarize my nearly 24 years of smoking journey, explaining how I progressed from smoking 2-3 puffs to consuming around twenty cigarettes per day by 2023-24.

As you can see, I didn't develop this habit overnight; it took years. During this time, nicotine wasn't the only reason it became difficult to quit; there were other major factors such as the perceived benefits, the reward system, and the incessant cravings.

As you read about my smoking journey, I hope it brings back memories of when you started this habit. Understanding your own journey is crucial if you're considering quitting. I'll guide you through how to use this journey to help you quit smoking as we continue together in this book.

Is Quitting Really Difficult? My Unsuccessful Attempts to Quit Smoking: A Reflection

Methods I attempted but ultimately proved ineffective.

Is Quitting Really Difficult? My Unsuccessful Attempts to Quit Smoking: A Reflection

Is quitting smoking difficult? Yes, it's comparable to any other bad habit one may have. We often observe people around us with various bad habits, most of which develop over time through repetition and become deeply ingrained in our subconscious minds. These habits typically come with their own rewards system and perceived benefits, which can vary from person to person.

Furthermore, addictions to substances like nicotine and alcohol exacerbate the challenge of quitting, as our bodies become accustomed to them. These substances trigger chemical reactions in our bodies, further reinforcing the habit. Additionally, the **perceived benefits and rewards** associated with these habits contribute to their persistence, making them even harder to overcome.

If you were to ask me which of these four factors—**addictions to substances, perceived benefits, rewards system, or feelings of loneliness—is the most difficult to overcome, based on my experience,** I would say that the

rewards system and feelings of loneliness play a significant role. While addictions to substances and perceived benefits can be managed, overcoming the first two factors is crucial for success.

Now let me share the methods I've attempted to quit smoking over the last 23 years, most of which unfortunately failed. I gleaned insights from the internet, books, and sought advice from individuals who had successfully quit.

The first method I tried was **Cold Turkey**, a widely recognized technique to quit smoking, approximately twelve years ago. For those unfamiliar, "**Cold Turkey**" means quitting smoking abruptly, relying solely on **willpower**, without gradual reduction or support.

In this approach, you make a firm decision to quit smoking abruptly, never touching another cigarette thereafter. You rely on sheer willpower and inform everyone around you about your decision, seeking their support to refrain from indulging in this habit again. While it's a commendable technique, it demands a considerable amount of willpower and energy. However, it often goes against the principle of conserving energy for maximum results. In this method, your entire energy is directed towards resisting

smoking cravings, leaving little to no energy for other daily tasks at home and in the office.

I gave my best effort and managed to refrain from smoking for approximately 35 days, but those days were incredibly challenging for me. I found it difficult to concentrate on anything, plagued by intense smoking cravings and feeling consistently low throughout the day. As a result, my performance both at work and at home suffered. Most of my energy was expended on resisting the urge to smoke through sheer willpower, leaving me feeling drained and ineffective.

During those 35 days, I felt a noticeable lack of excitement. I struggled to find motivation for tasks such as going to the office, delivering presentations to clients, writing emails, or attending office parties. These activities, which would typically bring me satisfaction, felt dull and uninspiring without the reward of a cigarette afterward.

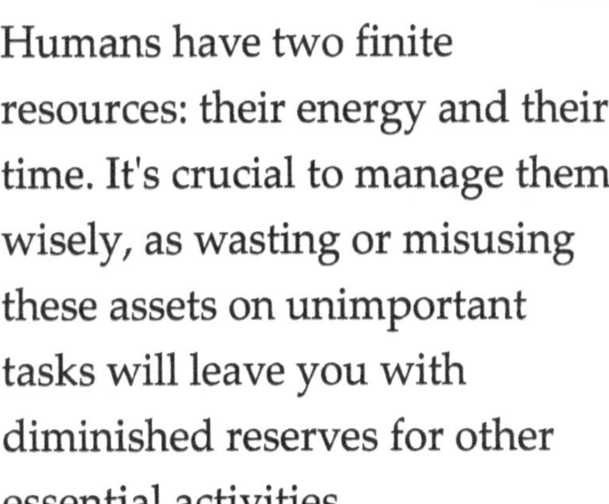

Humans have two finite resources: their energy and their time. It's crucial to manage them wisely, as wasting or misusing these assets on unimportant tasks will leave you with diminished reserves for other essential activities.

If a task requires a lot of energy, it's difficult to sustain it for an extended period. This was exactly what happened to me.

One fine day I was under immense pressure due to some office work and found it challenging to concentrate. Before I knew it, I found myself at the cigarette shop, lighting up again. In just five minutes, all the efforts I had put into quitting over the last 35 days vanished. I was back to smoking, although the taste wasn't as enjoyable, and it somehow reminded me of the first time I smoked. However, my mind and body felt relieved after that cigarette, almost as if nicotine had worked its magic.

I felt terrible afterward, wondering why I had succumbed and why I couldn't control myself. After finishing the cigarette and berating myself, I returned to my desk and resumed work. Interestingly, I found that I could concentrate better on my tasks. My mind seemed convinced that it no longer needed to expend energy resisting the urge to smoke since I had already indulged. While I didn't complete all my work, I managed to make progress and felt satisfied for the day.

On my way home, I rewarded myself with another cigarette for the progress I had made at work. Simultaneously, I couldn't shake the feeling of disappointment in myself for giving in and resuming smoking. I attempted to limit myself to just one or two cigarettes daily, only when I felt the need most, believing that this would reduce the harm compared to smoking 10 cigarettes a day. However, this strategy proved ineffective, and within 10 to 15 days, I found myself back at square one, where I had started with the Cold Turkey method and by this first attempt to quit smoking failed.

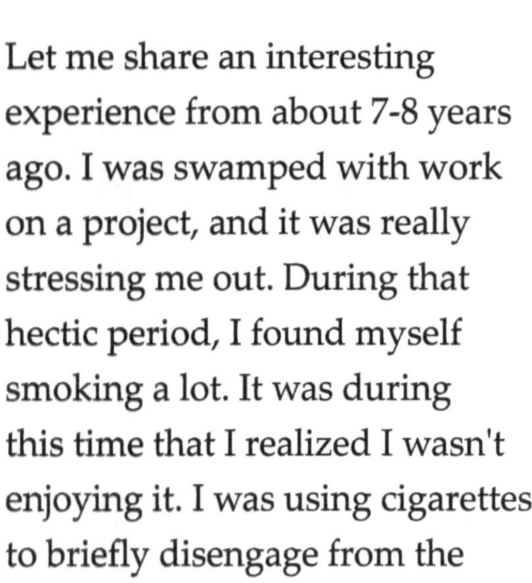

Let me share an interesting experience from about 7-8 years ago. I was swamped with work on a project, and it was really stressing me out. During that hectic period, I found myself smoking a lot. It was during this time that I realized I wasn't enjoying it. I was using cigarettes to briefly disengage from the project, but it was impacting my ability to concentrate fully. I found myself taking smoking breaks every 15-30 minutes, which some of my peers found annoying. This was the first time I noticed the bed smell of cigarette from my hands and experienced a very dry mouth. I was not able to enjoy even some delicious food or beverages felt like my all-test bud are dead due to extensive smoking.

However, once the project concluded, I took a hiatus and returned to hometown for a month to relax. Spending time with my parents brought about a significant change. I found that

I no longer had the same craving for cigarettes as before. Perhaps it was because I had indulged heavily in the previous month, and now my body was rejecting it. I relished the meals prepared by my mother and being away from the workplace made it easier to resist the urge to smoke. During those 30 days, I scarcely smoked at all, and it felt effortless. It was as if my willpower didn't even need to intervene—it happened naturally.

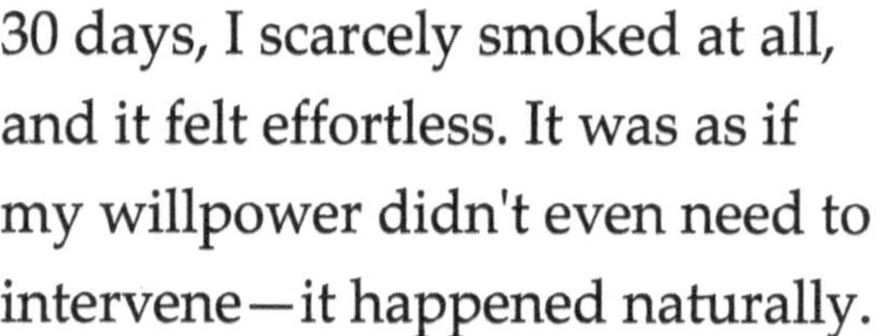

I was very surprised at how I managed to survive effortlessly for a month in my hometown by just smoking 1-2 cigarettes, whereas it would have been quite difficult for me if I tried to quit cold turkey.

Then, I realized what was missing - the triggers that signal me to smoke. The surroundings in which we live were absent here, as I was living with my parents and away from the group of smokers.

Secondly, there was no need for a rewards system here, as I wasn't doing any office or minimal household work. Most of the things were taken care of by my father, or they were done in a planned manner without any stress. So, my mind was relaxed and already in a good state, not seeking any additional reward or momentary relief in the form of smoking.

Then, I concluded that it is easier to manage nicotine cravings when you are away from the surroundings that trigger your urge to smoke. However, the most difficult aspect was the reward system that was ingrained in my mind, where I would reward myself with smoking after accomplishing or starting any task.

However, as soon as I returned to the workplace within 4-5 days, I resumed my old routine of enjoying cigarettes with my well-known group and indulging in the perceived benefits and rewards system.

After two years, the idea of quitting crossed my mind when

I learned that one of my old friends had successfully quit using Nicotine Gums. That very day, I bought a packet of the best nicotine gums tailored to my cigarette intake.

I used it for a couple of days, and initially, my cigarette count reduced a bit as the gum provided the required nicotine, but 3 things were still missing - the reward and perceived benefits, and a momentary relief or detachment from the current situation, which I got from smoking. After a week, I found myself smoking while chewing nicotine gum, essentially taking a double dose of nicotine, one

from smoking and another from
the gum.

I found this method totally
ineffective, so I quit...
**Smoking? No way! Only
nicotine gum
for me**

Another effort to
stop smoking proved
unsuccessful, and I found
myself smoking for years without
giving quitting much thought.
Then, one day, my friend arrived
in Delhi from the United States,
where he was based. It had been
long time since our last encounter,
and when he departed, he, too,
was a smoker.

We used to smoke and drink beers
in his car when he was in NCR.
Smoking and drinking in the car

were seen as a status symbol and a fashionable trend during that era, particularly in NCR (I don't promote it but I enjoy it without disturbing others)

Over the years, I had also purchased a small car, and this time I invited him to join me in my car to reminisce about our old days. I eagerly picked him up from his home in my car, which was stocked with beers and a pack of cigarettes. Our plan was to enjoy our time together, savouring the drinks and cigarettes, while catching up on his experiences in the US.

As soon as he boarded my car, I offered him a chilled beer. You'll be surprised to know how I offered him chilled beer. In those years, I also evolved like others who enjoy one or two beers peacefully in their own car, either parked or at favourite roadside food spots. Therefore, my car was equipped with all the amenities required for smoking and drinking. I named it 'KAROBAR' in Hindi, which means 'Business.' If you break down this word, it becomes CAR-O-BAR, indicating a bar in the car. So, I also had a chilled box in my car filled with ice and beers, allowing us to enjoy chilled beer inside the car. He was very happy to see all these arrangements, and I proudly accepted his appreciation.

After a few sips of beer,
I offered my friend a cigarette
from a new pack I had bought
for the occasion.
Surprisingly, he declined,
mentioning he had quit
smoking two years
prior. I was taken aback,
wondering how he
managed it, especially
since he was a heavier
smoker when he left for the USA
four years ago.

I was amazed when he pulled
out an electronic cigarette
and started vaping. Curious,
I decided to give it a shot
myself. While the sensation
was like smoking, it wasn't
quite the same. After discussing
his success with vaping, I

became convinced that it might be the solution I needed to quit smoking.

Determined to make the switch, I requested an electronic cigarette and refills from my friend. With his help, I started vaping exclusively, determined to break free from smoking. From that day forward, I left cigarettes behind and embraced vaping as a healthier alternative.

The following day, I delved into research about vaping, exploring its pros and cons. Surprisingly, I found compelling evidence that it could be an effective tool for quitting smoking. Encouraged by this discovery, I ordered a few refills and began my vaping journey.

As anticipated, vaping closely resembled smoking and offered similar perceived benefits. However, I soon encountered a hurdle: the inconvenience of carrying vaping equipment everywhere. This realization dawned on me after a period of struggling with the logistics, compounded by the sceptical glances from fellow smokers who viewed vaping with suspicion. These experiences left me feeling awkward and unsure about continuing with vaping.

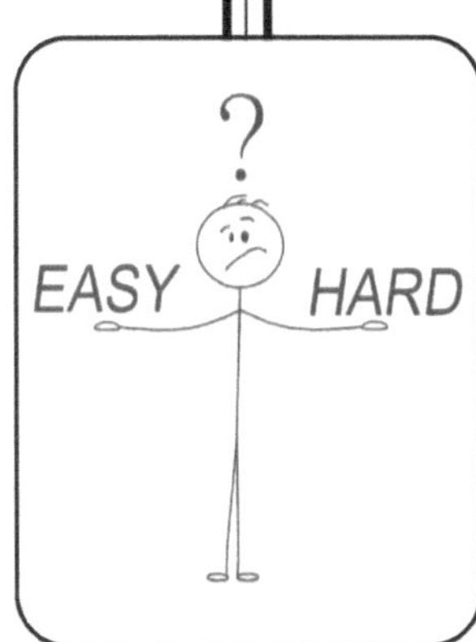

I kept vaping for about two months without smoking, but then I went back to smoking. It was too much hassle to carry vaping stuff all the time, and getting refills was tricky because they weren't widely available or legal in India at that time.

Following that, I embarked on further attempts employing alternative strategies & managed to quit smoking for some period. But despite making progress, I found myself drawn back to smoking once more.

Now, when asked the best way to quit, I say it depends on the person. While some may succeed with those methods, they didn't work for me. I don't call them useless; they just didn't work for me.

In the upcoming chapter, I'll guide you through crafting your personal quit plan. I'll offer advice to steer you in the right direction, but remember, you're the one who must steer your own path through the challenges of quitting smoking.

Where to Start?

Simple steps to begin your journey
to quit smoking.

Where to Start?

I'm sure you're eagerly anticipating this chapter, wondering what extraordinary insights this guy is going to share with us. Well, before we dive in, let me share some thought that I came across and kept in mind when naming my book "Don't Quit Smoking, Just Drop One Cigarette."

Whenever you want to start or quit a habit, it's important to have a clear end goal in mind and plan to achieve it. There's an interesting theory behind this: if you want to reach a destination, you must take the first step towards it.

Let me illustrate with an example. Imagine you're determined to achieve six-pack abs, so you decide to join a gym. The beauty of the mind is that when we think about a goal and plan, it gives us internal satisfaction

and makes us feel like we're making progress. Your aim is to achieve a six-pack, leading you to choose to join a gym. However, upon investigation and careful selection, you discover that the monthly gym membership is costly.

But if you opt for the yearly plan, it seems more affordable. However, you'll need to pay the entire amount upfront. Now, suppose you already in the middle of the month and can't afford it, you decide to join the gym starting next month once you receive your salary. After 15 days, you have enough funds to

join the gym, but you realize that you can't join without proper shoes and a tracksuit.

You spend the entire day searching for the best shoes and tracksuit for the gym, but they turn out to be expensive. Since you've already reserved the monthly fee for your yearly membership, you can't afford to spend money on shoes and a tracksuit. So, you decide to save the yearly fee this month and use your salary from the next month to buy the selected tracksuit and shoes and start going to the gym.

Have you noticed something?

Your mind may give you satisfaction that you're making progress towards your goal of achieving a six-pack. However, despite your planning, you haven't made any progress. On the very first day that you desired to have a six-pack, if you had started by doing just one or two push-ups, in the last two months that you've spent only desiring and planning, you could have completed at least fifty push-ups or even more. This would have at least moved you a bit closer to your six-pack goal.

The principle also applies to quitting smoking. Your goal is to quit

altogether, so begin by reducing your daily intake by at least one cigarette. Take it one day at a time. Enjoy the journey as you gradually cut back, and you'll find that things naturally fall into place, requiring less willpower and energy.

Another significant aspect of quitting smoking is overcoming the rewards system, perceived advantages, momentary relief, and nicotine cravings. In the next chapter, I will delve into how you can create your own personalized quitting strategy. Each person's journey is unique, so I'll provide

both a map and a compass. While the map is essential, the compass is crucial for reaching your destination efficiently and with fewer obstacles.

Creating a Quit Plan

Emphasizing the importance of having a plan for success.

Creating a Quit Plan

Let's dive into the most anticipated chapter. But before we begin, **I want to make it clear that I don't hold any professional degree, and the methods discussed here have only been tested by me**. They've proven to be effective for me, but results may vary for others. I encourage you to give them a try and find what works best for you in your journey to quit smoking.

As discussed in earlier pages, this plan addresses factors beyond nicotine that make quitting challenging. Let me quickly summarize them for clarity:

1. Perceived Benefits – Hidden advantages that you perceive from smoking.
2. Reward System in the Mind – The habit of needing a cigarette before and after completing tasks.
3. Temporary Escape from Reality – Momentary relief from tense situations.
4. Sense of Companionship – Feeling accompanied without judgment.
5. Nicotine Cravings – Chemical reactions in the body that prompt the urge to smoke.

My quit plan is built on the challenges and issues I faced while trying other proven methods available in the market.

Remember, don't disclose to anyone that you're working on quitting smoking. Act like a regular smoker outwardly, but internally, follow the quit plan. This way, you'll still feel like part of the smoking group and enjoy the **perceived benefits** while working towards quitting.

If someone close to you also wants to quit, you can both quietly start following the plan together. Talking about how it's going can help support each other and make you feel better and engaged.

Let's approach this like we're project managers and see quitting smoking as a challenge. Enjoy the journey of quitting and regularly review your progress. If you find yourself straying from the plan or falling behind, apply your techniques to get back on track.

Step 1 – Count the number of cigarettes you smoke per day.

Why:

- Slowly transition this smoking habit from unconscious to conscious awareness. When you count the number of cigarettes you smoke, you engage your conscious mind.

How:

- Use a whiteboard or mobile device to track the number

of cigarettes and the time for each day. At night, tally the total when you smoke your last cigarette for the day. Ensure it remains visible to you throughout the day.

Till When:

- Repeat this for at least 30 days and make it a habit to count the number of cigarettes per day. Total them per week and then per month. If you're concerned about finances, calculate how much you spend. If not, skip this step.

  (People have advised me that if I invest the 4K/month which I spend on cigarettes into an

SIP with a 12% ROI for the past 24 years, I would have accumulated 50 lakhs, enabling me to purchase a BMW. While their advice is sound, it's interesting to note that they themselves do not adhere to it, nor do they own a BMW)

- Remember, if for any reason you can't count one day, do it the next day, but don't go more than two days without counting. To make counting as a habit varies for everyone. One thing to remember: **don't smoke before you count or write it down.**

Step 2 – Set a maximum number of cigarettes you can smoke per day and maintain it.

o   Now, I believe in tracking your daily cigarette intake as part of your routine. By doing so, you can determine how many cigarettes you typically smoke per day and at what times.

Why:

- To understand the patterns influencing our smoking habits, transitioning information from our subconscious to conscious mind.

How:

- Based on this data, establish a daily limit for cigarettes. For instance, if the average is 20 cigarettes per day over 14 hours (excluding 10 hours for sleep or other essential activities without smoking), divide these 20 cigarettes across the 14-hour period to create a plan like the one below:

20 Cigarettes Per Day = Max Limit		
8-10 AM	11 AM - 8 PM	9 PM - 11:30 PM
4 Cigarettes	11 Cigarettes	5 Cigarettes

- Don't buy a whole pack of cigarettes; instead, get only what you plan to smoke. For example, if you usually smoke four cigarettes between 8 AM and 10 AM, just buy or take out four cigarettes for that time. This method helps you stick to your set limit. Remember, it's based on how many cigarettes you usually smoke during certain time.

Till When

- Do this for the next two months; gradually increase your self-control. You're now beginning to learn how to control your cigarette consumption, rather than letting cigarettes control you.

- It is fine if 1 day you smoke more or not follow the plan but make sure you stick with the plan for next day.

Step 3 - Drop One Cigarette only from your daily consumption.

o I believe you've been sticking to the agreed-upon intake count so far and have been following it consistently for at least 2 months, with only 1-2 minor slip-ups, which is perfectly fine.

Why:

- We are now beginning to backtrack the journey of smoking. From this point, you must trace back to the stage where you first experienced it.

How:

- Choose a time when cravings are minimal and "Drop just one cigarette" from your daily routine. Keep track of this change.

Till When:

- Maintain this reduced count for the next 15 days or more. If successful, drop one or two more cigarettes each day, gradually reducing your intake. Remember to track your progress daily and stay consistent.

*Tips:

As you're still smoking, albeit less, and nobody knows you're trying to quit, they still assume you're a smoker, so you still experience the perceived benefits of smoking. Another important aspect is rewiring your brain's ingrained reward system associated with smoking and finding a momentary detachment from the current situation. To address this, from now on, before you take your smoke break, whether to reward yourself or for a moment of detachment, start by having a cup of tea, chocolate, a glass of water, or a healthy snack. Alternatively, engage in any other enjoyable activity such as checking social media, listening to a song, or talking to your girlfriend for 2-3 minutes before lighting your cigarette. This can help break the automatic association between smoking and reward, gradually reshaping your habits.

Step 4 – Now Use the Cold Turkey Method (for 1 day Only)

- o If you've reached this stage and still adhered to the plan, then you're on the right path. By now, I believe you've reduced your daily cigarette intake by at least 5-8 cigarettes and maintained that count for about a month. Additionally, you've been rewarding yourself or finding other means of detachment before lighting a cigarette. I'm confident that you now have good control over this habit, enjoying it only when you want or have planned, rather than anytime, anywhere.

Why:

– Up to this point, we've successfully reduced our intake and gained control over it, while also practicing alternative activities for rewarding and detachment alongside smoking. Now, it's important to assess how much willpower is required to abstain from smoking for a day.

How:

- Decide to go without smoking for one day while still taking cigarette breaks to detach and reward yourself. Engage in other activities, like those developed in earlier steps.

- I'm certain that if you take breaks without cigarettes, you'll experience fewer cravings since the other activities are in place, and you've only removed cigarettes.

Till When:

- If possible, repeat this process for four weeks, selecting one day each week to not smoke.

On the remaining days, maintain your reduced cigarette count. If possible, extend the duration of not smoking to two or three days depending on your will power.

Step 5 – Drop the last one.

o If you've followed the plan for six months, you've managed to reverse the journey. However, for others, you may still be perceived as a smoker, so you'll continue to reap the perceived advantages. You've already found alternatives for rewards and detachment.

o   Just remember, you weren't born a smoker; before you started smoking, you had other means to reward and detach yourself from situations.

o   Smoking is an alternative you developed over time, which is detrimental to your health and your wallet. In this reverse journey, you just need to recall the days when you didn't smoke and see that you can live without it.

o   Now, the final step is to drop the last cigarette easily without any impact on your mindset. By this time, you've truly learned how to live without smoking. But don't label yourself as a non-smoker from now on; instead, enjoy the company of smokers without feeling the need to have a cigarette. Even if you take 1-2 puffs in a month, remember how you felt when you smoked for the first time and cursed yourself.

o I personally followed the above-mentioned steps and was able to quit smoking without experiencing any side effects. I still enjoy the company of smokers. You can modify and tweak these steps according to your behaviour. So, best of luck! I know you can do it.

One final point I'd like to share with you before concluding this chapter on the perceived benefits we derive from smoking.

Reflecting on life at 44, I can't help but think about the journey from my twenties to my forties. Life presents different challenges, like completing academic degrees, finding the right job, or true love.

As you get married, more responsibilities come your way: managing your relationship, work-life balance, buying a new car or house, and caring for aging parents. Despite the chaos, there's a resilience that emerges—the ability to persevere and overcome obstacles.

The perceived benefits of smoking, whether in college or professionally, play a critical role in our twenties to forties, making it challenging to quit. However, by the time we reach forty, things start to change. Responsibilities become more manageable, and the need for cigarettes diminishes.

At this stage, our circle of friends changes too. They support us for who we are, not our habits. With their presence, the allure of smoking fades, and we may consider returning to the simplicity of our youth.

For those still smoking past forty, it's a moment of reflection—a chance to reconsider the journey ahead. Perhaps it's time to rediscover who we were before cigarettes clouded our vision.

The Journey's End: Celebrating Smoke-Free Success

Summarizing the key points & additional resources for support.

The Journey's End: Celebrating Smoke-Free Success

It's truly surprising to find myself at this stage of completing this book. When I began, doubts lingered about my ability to see it through. Nonetheless, my aim was to share my journey of quitting smoking with fellow smokers. I hope that by sharing my experiences, it may offer guidance to those seeking to break free from this habit.

Reflecting on my smoking journey, I can acknowledge moments of enjoyment. Those unfamiliar with it may not grasp what they've overlooked in life. However, there came a point where I reached my limit. Quitting wasn't pleasurable; it became a necessary change as smoking had become deeply ingrained in my daily routine.

Presently, I feel a newfound sense of relaxation. Social gatherings, train and flight journeys, and meals are now enjoyed more peacefully. The worry of finding a place to smoke or ensuring I have enough cigarettes is no longer a concern. Quitting has gifted me a sense of freedom and tranquillity that I hadn't realized was absent.

Throughout this journey, I've cultivated new habits, such as reading books during my free time and hitting the gym. I drew inspiration from various sources, including books like Atomic Habits, The

Power of Your Subconscious Mind, I am time by Deep Trivedi and others whose titles elude me at present.

This is based on my own journey and some principles that I find very useful in our day-to-day lives. Firstly, you need to convince yourself that you want to quit for yourself, not for others. Start with small, achievable targets that require less energy & will power like dropping only 1 cigarette.

Two things are limited in this world: time and energy. If your target goals seem

unachievable, such as quitting in one shot (Cold Turkey), it will require a lot of energy, and you may not be able to sustain it for long. Therefore, always aim for small goals that are 4% above what you currently have. In this approach, start by reducing your intake by just one cigarette and gradually make it a habit. When an action becomes a habit, it requires very little energy and becomes automatic.

Secondly, consider the concepts of **"Chesta – Desire" and "Karama – Actions".** As humans, we desire many things, and the beauty of desire

is that it only gives perception to your mind that you are doing something to fulfil that desire. For example, quitting smoking is a desire; you think about it, discuss it with others, watch videos, and read books like the one you are currently reading. However, do not take any action, or karma, towards it, at least initially. Take your first step towards quitting by dropping one cigarette.

As I conclude this book, I am profoundly grateful to you for taking the time to read it. Whether you have found success in quitting smoking with the help of this book or have developed

your own customized method, I would be overjoyed to hear about your journey. Please don't hesitate to reach out to **journeytaleslk@gmail.com** and share your experience.

Thank you, and I wholeheartedly believe that anyone can achieve success in quitting smoking, as **you are not born with cigarettes.**